WILD YORKSHIRE

WILD YORKSHIRE

IN ASSOCIATION WITH YORKSHIRE WILDLIFE TRUST

First published in Great Britain 2002 by
Dalesman Publishing Company Limited
Stable Courtyard
Broughton Hall
Skipton
North Yorkshire BD23 3AZ
www.dalesman.co.uk

Introduction © David Bellamy
Main text © Yorkshire Wildlife Trust
Photographs © Mike Coultas, Mark Hamblin, Mike Kipling, Helen Kirk,
Ken Paver, Laurie Ramsay, Colin Raw, Ian Robinson, Denis and Mary Sykes,
David Tarn, Jon Traill

A British Cataloguing in Publication record is available for this book

ISBN 185568 202 8

Designed by Jonathan Newdick
Colour Origination by Grasmere Digital Imaging Limited
Printed by Midas Printing (HK) Limited

Overleaf. The North York Moors
near Egton Bridge.

CONTENTS

INTRODUCTION BY DAVID BELLAMY
PRESIDENT OF THE WILDLIFE TRUSTS

Thwaite in upper Swaledale typifies the vernacular architecture of the limestone dales. A cluster of old farm houses and cottages nestle in the valley bottom beside the bridge over the beck. For generations sheep have grazed the surrounding moors throughout summer, leaving flower-rich meadows in the valley to bloom before being cut for hay.

I had of course seen Yorkshire with all its ridings on the map and had wondered as to its history and its size, long before I made my first trip back in the late forties – leaving London up what was then called The Great North Road in an ex-police Wolseley. Back in those days it was a slow journey along mainly single carriageway roads, a meandering transect across England in all her biodiverse glory. Mind you, we didn't call it biodiversity then, we called it wildflowers and wildlife and it was there in plenty. Small farms, with small fields edged with well laid hedgerows, lots of farm workers with little grey tractors and even horses working in the fields; estates both large and small run by game-keepers, each one a natural historian in his own right, and farmers' wives who could pick a wealth of wildflowers to adorn the altar on Sunday. The same pattern of this Rural Idyll, whatever that was, was repeated as we crossed the Yorkshire border and went on and on and on until we drove through the Vale of Pickering for our destination at Kirkleatham by Redcar. It was from there that I first saw the muck and brass of heavy industry still with fingers, not of monotonous green, but richly coloured flower-full meadows, pastures and fallow fields reaching down from the Moors. There too were what we now call brownfield sites in every stage of recolonisation by native and alien plants. The great River Tees polluted with sewage and a fricassee of chemicals that poured from many outfalls proved that the solution to pollution was not dilution. The demise of heavy industry was not far away, nor was the Common Agricultural Policy.

Although I didn't know it, Yorkshire Wildlife Trust or Naturalists' Trust as it was then known was already in existence and Askham Bog was its first nature reserve. As hedgerows began to fall and old spoil heaps, quarries and gravel pits became refugia for more and more of our

Askham Bog: the first reserve.

native flora and fauna, the Wildlife Trusts Partnership as it is now known began to come into being. Experts in every field of natural history were beginning to see more and more countryside threatened by massive change and so took up the challenge. They became the real campaigners, not only by trying to stop things but by getting on with the job of protecting as many of the endangered habitats in their areas as they could get their expert fingers into. Today they are a dynamic partnership working together with farmers, landowners, businesses both great and small and government at all levels to put the whole of the British Isles back into more biodiverse working order.

Once I had metamorphosed from a schoolboy doing my level best to get qualifications in botany and zoology into a research student studying wetlands, mires and bogs, I just had to see Askham for it is the meeting of wetland plants typical of the warmer, dryer south-east and the wetter, cooler north-west. In this valley mire things like water violet and bog myrtle grow cheek by jowl and the buzz of happy insects and the sight of birds and bats feeding on them was, in modern speak, real cool. Askham is still in safe hands and the buzz of biodiversity is still there; sadly, other similar sites are gone. I was going to say "gone forever" but now, using our portfolio of reserves as banks of local genetic diversity, the Trust is hard at work rehabilitating other areas.

Spurn Point at the mouth of the Humber is another haven for both wildlife and naturalists. An important stopover and refuelling site along the migration routes through the North Sea, this chalk and clay ridge hooks both birds and twitchers in great numbers. The maritime vegetation is also of great importance for it holds this flyway service station together, one hopes, whatever the vagaries of global warming fling its way. Management includes both dealing with the increasing number of people who want to come and see it all for themselves and the viability of the vegetation and natural processes that keep it all in place. A real battle fit for King Canute, but the Trust has all the experts and lots of willing volunteers on its side.

Two very different reserves are Potteric Carr and Wheldrake Ings for both were people made and people managed long before Yorkshire Wildlife Trust became a key player in the process.

Potteric is perhaps the most public of all reserves because the main railway line between Scotland and London runs alongside it on an embankment that in part helped in its creation. I see it many times every year as the train begins to slow down or speed up in and out of Doncaster Station. There is always something to see – birds resting, nesting or feeding from the water and the reed swamp, great clouds of insects including a range of damsel- and dragonflies shimmering in the sunlight. Even in the evening it is possible to see owls hawking in the moonlight. In late spring a transformation of part of the smaller ponds takes place as the armoured leaves of the water soldier rise up from their winter sleep in the depths to flower floating on the surface. All this appeared to be in danger thanks to plans to build a major road. Potteric is still doing fine and the dawn chorus can still be heard – a success story of real conservation.

To a botanist Wheldrake Ings is a heaven on earth, one of Britain's last remaining hay meadows on seasonally flooded neutral soils. If that sounds boring to you well it isn't – it is a living patchwork of flowers all of which are allowed to set seed before more than one man comes and mows the meadow. Yes, meadows are people made and people managed and as 98 per cent of Britain's flower-rich grasslands have disappeared thanks to mismanagement over the past 40 years these communities are of international importance. It's not only conservationists who enjoy the summer spectacle but so do skylarks, lapwing, redshank and occasionally lekking ruff. When in the winter the River Derwent overflows its banks the flooded meadows attract vast numbers of waders and wildfowl on their winter holidays or just passing through.

WOW! Wildlife on the wing – birds, butterflies and bats, with a carpet of wildflowers alive with insects and stands of native woodland all in the expert care of the local experts. Enough to cheer the hearts of old-time stalwarts of the Trust like Eva Crackles and the late William Bunting.

There are already another 82 Trust reserves in Yorkshire and more in the planning pipeline. Take a look in this superb book which takes you on a journey through the wildness of Yorkshire and if, when you've finished, you feel you would like to help conserve and promote all these wonders, then join the Wildlife Trust. Your life will never be the same again – all those reserves to enjoy with lots of opportunities to volunteer and work alongside the experts learning fascinating facts all the time.

Wordsworth called the smart little stonechat a 'restless bird' as it will fly busily within a small area. When it does stay still it will often flick its tail and sing for a short while. The song is like pebbles striking together, so old Yorkshire folk gave it the name stone clink. It's smaller than a house sparrow but much more striking.

YORKSHIRE WILDLIFE TRUST

Wheldrake Ings is one of our last great seasonal flood meadows, internationally important for its rich hay meadows and wintering birds

The Yorkshire Wildlife Trust has been working since 1946 'to conserve and promote the diversity of Yorkshire wildlife and habitats for the benefit and well-being of both wildlife and people'.

Many people think of conservation charities as just looking after nature reserves and the Trust looks after many valuable sites. But it also has a wider role in promoting recognition of wildlife issues and their importance to life in Yorkshire. The scope and importance of this work continues to grow as wildlife habitats, their plants and animals, are under increasing threat.

The nature reserves are spread throughout the county from Southerscales in the west to Spurn in the east, from Little Beck Wood in the north to Woodhouse Washlands in the south. On Trust reserves, land can be managed for the maximum benefit to wildlife and disturbance minimised. Habitats can be improved or created for the benefit of wild flowers and trees, migrating and breeding birds, lichens and lizards, badgers and beetles. They are also great places for people – to enjoy the landscape.

Many willing volunteers help look after these reserves and more volunteers are always welcome, however much or little time they can spare. This is just part of the Trust's efforts to involve more people with wildlife. Wildlife Watch Groups all over Yorkshire introduce young people to conservation, making learning fun and helping them join in practical projects, building ponds, planting wild flower meadows or doing surveys. So many people and organisations can have an effect on wildlife. Yorkshire Wildlife Trust tries to influence as many as possible to think of wildlife, protect it and make their plans with conservation in mind.

WATER FOR WILDLIFE

A donation from sales of this book will be made to Yorkshire Wildlife Trust's Water For Wildlife appeal.

The Trust's nature reserves include great wetland habitats from Semerwater in the Dales to Burton Riggs on the coast, from Bolton-on-Swale Lake in North Yorkshire to Potteric Carr in Doncaster. But the Trust's efforts to protect wildlife and water habitats stretch way beyond these reserves.

Yorkshire's wide range of wetland habitats – rivers, canals, lakes, ponds, fens and flood plains – offers huge potential for wildlife including otters, water voles, dragonflies, sand martins and kingfishers.

The Water for Wildlife Project works for all these species, monitoring where they are, advising land owners, carrying out practical work and campaigning right across Yorkshire.

Historically otters and water voles bred throughout the county but there was a severe decline during the 1960s and '70s. Ninety-eight per cent of the water vole population was lost. Over the past 10 years, Yorkshire Wildlife Trust has achieved a great deal, encouraging the return of otters to their former range. There are sightings on many of our rivers, in towns, cities and the countryside and they spread further every year. Water voles are being helped as well and there are more positive signs.

The positive news does not just concern wildlife. Without the commitment of people, little can be achieved. It is very encouraging that so many are willing to help and the Trust has been the catalyst for the successful involvement of local people, from landowners to volunteers. Many farmers and landowners wish to help wildlife and will adapt their plans if they can help species like water voles. Enthusiasts have learnt about otters, so they can look for field signs, carry out surveys and provide essential information.

There is much more to be done and it is vital that the success over the last few years is built on. You can help our work by joining the Yorkshire Wildlife Trust. Membership benefits include our colour magazine three times a year, access to our nature reserves and the chance to come to special events. Plus the knowledge that you really are protecting Yorkshire's wildlife.

For more information please contact the Yorkshire Wildlife Trust: telephone 01904 659570, e-mail info@yorkshirewt.cix.co.uk or visit www.yorkshire-wildlife-trust.org.uk

The banded demoiselle is just one of many countless species which depend on Yorkshire's wetland areas for survival. It needs a slow flow of water, with good vegetation round the water's edge.

Coast

Gulls are one of the most successful species at exploiting the man-made landscape. These herring gulls have found a convenient perch on which to rest and it's likely that almost every man-made structure along the coast will have been visited by a bird at some time. But gulls have moved closer to humans and their townscapes in other ways. They will nest on houses, not just at the coast but well inland, and feed among tips and landfill sites which are now a regular haunt for bird-watchers keen to spot rare species, such as an Iceland or a glaucous gull, among the huge flocks which gather there.

Yorkshire's coast provides a wonderful range of habitats for wildlife, from the dramatic sweep of the Boulby cliffs in the north to the flat salt-marsh and mud flats of the Humber estuary in the south.

Most wildlife habitats are the result of man's impact on the landscape; but on the coast things are different. Man has had to adapt to the landscape rather than it to man.

Cliffs are the preserve of seabirds in spring, as they find nest sites on the narrowest of ledges, providing some of the county's easiest and most exciting wildlife watching. Man must go where the formation of the coast allows access to the shore. There are landings used for launching boats around the chalk cliffs of Flamborough Head but most of the coastline is inaccessible and a safe haven for breeding seabirds in their thousands.

Further south, the sea again is in control. From Filey to Spurn Point, where sea and sand dominate, coastal erosion is a defining feature. The lower cliffs are continually worn away by the North Sea, as storms wash more and more of the county into the sea. The Spurn peninsula which stretches three-and-a-half miles into the Humber estuary is made up of debris washed down by the action of wind and water from the crumbling cliffs to the north.

Every storm threatens to punch a hole through Spurn, and this provides a clear example of how erosion, global warming and rising sea levels are increasing the threat to the area. There are difficult decisions to be made on how to cope with Yorkshire's changing coastline.

Black-headed gulls are one of many mis-named birds. Their heads are chocolate brown during the breeding season and white during winter. Often called seagulls, black-headed gulls, like many other species, are found inland as well as on the coast.

Man has been unable to tame the force of the sea but birds are perfectly adapted to coping with waves, such as these at Boulby, feeding offshore all year round. Apart from during the breeding season, they spend most of their lives far from land. The swell of the North Sea doesn't stop them searching for the shoals of fish on which they prey.

Yorkshire is probably the best county in which to see the magnificent gannet as it nests on cliffs near Flamborough and Bempton. The bright yellow of the head is particularly deep in the breeding season and, combined with black wing-tips, makes the gannet unmistakeable. The plumage develops over three years; younger birds are grey.

Gannets usually pair for life, breeding from their fourth or fifth year. Pairs have distinctive exchange sequences to strengthen their bond – raising their wings and spreading their tails, bowing, pointing at the sky and lowering their bill to the other's breast. Since nest sites can be in short supply, they are defended by both male and female.

Razorbills are difficult to see for much of the year, feeding far out to sea. They come to Yorkshire's cliffs to breed, usually choosing a narrow ledge on which to lay a single egg. Similar to guillemots, they are black, rather than dark chocolate, and have a bill shaped like an old-fashioned razor, hence their name.

Guillemots are a common sight on chalk cliffs. Unlike the razorbill, their bill is pointed. Gathering in dense colonies, they make no nests but lay a single egg on a flat surface – pear shaped to stop it rolling off. After about three weeks the young jump into the sea, still unable to fly. Here they are fed by a parent until they are old enough to dive from the surface to fish for themselves.

Flamborough Head is one of the most distinctive natural features on the Yorkshire coast and its high cliffs, with so many bays and inlets, make it a popular spot for a walk. Part of Flamborough is a Yorkshire Wildlife Trust Nature Reserve and in spring visitors can see thousands of breeding seabirds, including puffins, shags, razorbills and guillemots.

With a wing span of almost two metres, gannets are easy to spot in flight, cruising effortlessly over the North Sea. They can be seen making dives of up to 40 metres into the water, throwing their wings back just as they break the surface, complete masters of the air and sea. Their skulls are extra strong to resist the force of the water as they dive.

Right. Smaller and slimmer than the cormorant, shags are regularly seen flying close to the water, as they return to their cliff nests which are often on shady ledges slightly hidden from view. Unusual for seabirds, nest building is an important skill for a shag – if the nest is not well constructed, young can fall into the sea. It uses local materials, such as twigs and seaweed.

Below. The common tern is one of Yorkshire's most stylish birds, although many will be just passing through on their way to breeding grounds further north. Terns have a slimmer build than gulls and seem more skilful in flight. When they hunt, they tilt their heads forward and scan the water for food, often twisting and partially closing up their wings before diving.

Gulls soar over Staithes. This east coast fishing village nestles into cliffs where the beck tumbles down to the sea, protected from the ravages of North Sea gales.

There are over 80,000 grey seals living in and around our coast. They account for about one half of the world population and are therefore of international importance. In the autumn the seals congregate at traditional sites to breed. Pups will weigh around 14kg at birth and grow rapidly on their mother's rich milk – they can gain up to 2kg in weight each day.

The lighthouse dominates the sandy Spurn peninsula, a Yorkshire Wildlife Trust coastal reserve which stretches for three-and-a-half miles across the mouth of the River Humber. Spurn provides perfect opportunities for watching birds and their migration and offers much to interest the botanist: sea buckthorn dominates with lyme-grass, marram, sea-holly and sea rocket among the hundreds of species recorded.

Harebells, like the bellflowers of the same family, have been developed into a range of plants found in many Yorkshire gardens. Attractive, as well as easily identified, the native species needs no enhancement, especially when found alongside hawkweed, a combination which looks as good as many deliberate garden plantings.

Gulls collect on the Whitby shore for the twice daily ritual of following the falling tide. Sharp eyes and beaks seek out small marine creatures which have been too slow to hide beneath the protective sand. The weather of the North Sea has a fearsome reputation. Easterly gales frequently create crashing waves which send spume dozens of feet into the air as they strike the cliffs. Offshore windfarms may soon be harnessing this power to generate electricity.

Opposite. Filey Brigg, a slim finger of land at the end of the boulder-clay cliffs which stretch north towards Scarborough, is a favourite place for birdwatchers. Birds to spot include divers, shearwaters, gulls, ducks and waders. Sea-watching, with the wind blowing onto the shore, always offers the chance of spotting a rare species.

The purple sandpiper breeds in the far north but is seen regularly along the Yorkshire coast. It prefers to stop off on shores to feed, usually on seaweed-covered rocks, before heading to the tundra, sometimes breeding almost on the snowline.

Large flocks of sanderling gather on Yorkshire beaches during their passage north or in winter when they are resident. Flocks have a distinctive habit of racing along the beach together, very close to breaking waves. The plumage most commonly seen here is that of winter – white and grey.

Ravenscar seen from Boggle Hole, Robin Hood's Bay. The old water mill at Boggle Hole, lying in the bottom of a narrow steep-sided valley yards from the high tide line, could have made the perfect smugglers' landing beach. The outline of the Raven Hall Hotel, built on the site of a Roman signal station, sits atop the windswept cliffs, scarred with workings of old alum mines. The fossil-rich rocks abound in pools full of seaweed and marine life.

Another bird seen on passage through Yorkshire is the turnstone whose plumage has been described as looking like tortoiseshell. It feeds, as its name suggests, by using its bill to lift stones on rocky shores to get at marine life beneath, or by pulling back seaweed to expose prey.

The scale of the cliffs at Bempton never ceases to astonish. An RSPB reserve, it is the best place to see gannets, as here they nest on the coastal cliffs, rather than on their usual offshore islands. As well as these magnificent birds at close quarters, visitors can also see puffins and many other species. After the breeding season, though, the birds disperse to feed out at sea.

Brightly coloured bills make puffins one of the most distinctive and best-liked birds. The bills are used open and pointing upwards as a threatening display to rivals and in courtship which usually takes place at sea in large rafts of birds. Puffins can be seen offshore all year round but spring is the time to get the best views for they nest near the top of cliffs, in burrows or crevices.

Despite the harsh conditions along the coast, many wildflowers flourish, such as the pyramidal orchid and ox-eye daisy (top). The scarlet common poppy is a familiar sight throughout Yorkshire's countryside but the yellow-horned poppy (bottom) is found in a more specialised habitat near the coast. It grows on sea-cliffs, even in shingle and sands, in well-drained areas, though occasionally it can be found on waste ground further inland.

The Yorkshire coast is important for many migrating birds and areas of open water just inland also provide food for the migrants. Rare birds are regular at Hornsea Mere and lucky birdwatchers may see black tern or white-winged black tern. There is also a wide range of breeding species and many wildfowl visit in winter.

Heath and bog

Hatfield Moor in South Yorkshire is part of the Humberhead Peatlands, an area which also includes Thorne, Goole, Crowle and Rawcliffe Moors which are now sites of extreme importance for wildlife and its conservation. Hatfield Moor is the second largest lowland raised bog in Britain and contains rare beetle species found nowhere else in the UK.

In Yorkshire, peat habitats are usually associated with high moorland areas. However, while most of Britain's lowland peat bog is in Scotland and Ireland, with lowland heath mainly in the south of England, some of each lies in Yorkshire.

The vast tracts of Thorne and Hatfield Moors are examples of raised bogs, where the peat accumulates to levels higher than the surrounding countryside. The moors are the two largest lowland raised mires in Britain, covering a total of approximately 4000 hectares; more than 5500 species of insect have been recorded here – around 25 per cent of British fauna – including over 250 nationally scarce species. They form one of Britain's oldest habitats. Few bacteria survive in the acidic peat where there is minimal free oxygen, and this inhibits the process of decay allowing an archive of four millennia to be preserved. Charred tree stumps yield rare clues to the activities of Bronze Age communities. If the mire dries, this record is lost forever. These wonderful habitats are still threatened. Education is crucial to their survival and a recognition of their value other than as a horticultural resource is essential.

Heathland is usually comprised of a range of shrub species on a layer of peat – an important habitat, particularly for reptiles. Regular grazing, burning and clearance by man has kept heathland in a stable condition for centuries. Without this, a natural succession would have taken place, with larger trees and shrubs replacing grass, heather and scrub. This rare habitat can be seen at Yorkshire Wildlife Trust reserves at Allerthorpe Common and Strensall Common.

Askham Bog Nature Reserve features a rare combination of heath and bog where wetland plants such as bog myrtle grow alongside great fen sedge.

Ragged robin and marsh thistle take advantage of the richness of habitat at Askham Bog – the oldest Yorkshire Wildlife Trust reserve. A rare mix of fen and bog, Askham is renowned for its rare wetland plants and high species diversity.

Askham Bog is also a good place to see roe deer and Exmoor ponies sometimes graze here as part of an ongoing management conservation plan. The reserve is rich in insect life; some of its beetles and flies are found in very few other places. In the winter large flocks of redpoll and siskin join woodcock and lesser spotted woodpeckers that breed in summer.

Steam trains add drama to the landscape around Yorkshire Wildlife Trust's Fen Bog Nature Reserve. It lies in a wide valley, formed by glaciers, between Tom Cross Rigg and Crag Stone Rigg. Hikers pass through the reserve on the Lyke Wake Walk.

The elusive water rail is found in wetlands throughout Yorkshire but always where there is enough vegetation for it to hide safely, so its long red bill is rarely seen. Watched from some distance, the Yorkshire name rat hen looks appropriate but, close to, the olive-brown back with black spots, the black and white belly and the grey, almost lavender blue breast, give this tale the lie.

The nightjar often breeds on heaths and in forest clearings but, in Yorkshire, it is associated with ancient lowland peat bogs such as Thorne and Hatfield Moors. It is best known for its song – the unmistakable 'churring' can go on for hours, carrying up to a kilometre on a still evening – and for its wing-claps which form part of courtship. The nightjar hunts insects during the night, in a noiseless flight, sometimes with only the white patches on its wings showing up in the moonlight.

As the sundew grows in peaty bogs with little nutrient, it has to obtain all its food from small insects which get trapped by the sticky, red-coloured hairs on its leaves. These bend over securing the insect when it lands, and then excrete a digestive juice which dissolves the softer parts of the creature's body. This is then absorbed into the leaf.

Right. Sometimes called 'Ozzies', after the scientific name *Osmunda regalis*, the royal fern is among Europe's tallest fern, sometimes reaching over two metres in height. Askham Bog Nature Reserve is a good place to see them.

Below. Found on Yorkshire's fens and bogs, as well as wet heaths and moors, common butterwort is sometimes mistaken for a violet. The slender stems, without any leaves, flower in May and June.

The small pearl-bordered fritillary
is one of our rarer resident butterflies,
normally seen in June and July. In the
past it was found in many parts of
Yorkshire, but is now restricted to the
North Yorkshire Moors and the western
Pennines. It is found in damp grassland
or moorland areas where there are
violets, particularly marsh violets, on
which the caterpillars feed.

One of Yorkshire's rarest butterflies, the dark green fritillary is found in just a few places on the North Yorkshire Moors, and even fewer scattered Pennine sites. It flies between June and August in damp, grassy areas where violets grow. The caterpillars hibernate under dead grass and leaf litter as soon as they are hatched. They then feed on the violets when they wake up the following year.

HEATH AND BOG

Upland areas such as Egton Moor contain areas of bog which, though cursed by walkers, are welcomed by many species of wildlife. The North York Moors are one of the few places in Yorkshire where the large heath butterfly has been spotted. Also to be found are sphagnum moss, cotton grass and jointed rush as well as heather and bilberry which provide food for grouse.

Although the common lizard is no longer common in Yorkshire, it does have a wide range globally. It is hardy enough to survive close to the Arctic Circle and high in the Alps but is found on commons and heaths, in woodlands and hedgerows, and is sometimes seen basking in the sun. Its diet consists of small animals, particularly insects, spiders and grasshoppers. Most lizards lay eggs but common lizards give birth to live young, born in a thin membrane which they break through almost at once.

Left. There are over 2500 species of snake in the world but Great Britain has only three: the adder, the grass snake and the smooth snake. The grass snake, left, will swallow prey – such as frogs – alive and whole, separating bones in its jaw to open its mouth as wide as possible.

Below. Britain's only venomous snake is also the most common. Adders follow their prey by scent and use their venom to kill, sometimes living for a week on a single meal. They are easily identified by the strong diamond pattern on their back.

Many species of bog plant look very delicate, like sphagnum moss and polytrichum. Sphagnum is, in fact, a tough, spongy plant and forms cushions by drawing in water. As a result, it is popular with some gardeners as a liner for hanging baskets.

Bog asphodel is a dwarf lily-like plant which flourishes in boggy areas and wet flushes on hillsides. The bright yellow flowers in July and August, resembling a miniature gladiolus, turn to a rich red brown colour in the autumn.

At first glance, globeflowers look like buttercups but they are larger, a paler yellow and grow on taller stems. The yellow 'petals' which can be easily seen in July and August are in fact the outer parts of the flower; its sepals and the true flowers are hidden inside.

Purple loosestrife is easily spotted in damp ditches and along river banks by its long purple flower spikes in July and August. The strong, erect spikes and bright colour have made it a popular plant for the herbaceous border where it is known under its botanical name of *Lythrum*.

The longhorned beetle has yellow markings but is mainly black, with a long body. It feeds on pollen and is found among leaves of trees and shrubs, usually in summer.

There are many different species of the sand wasp, a solitary creature, which digs burrows in sand. Each has its own preferred habitat. Some place a large caterpillar in each burrow before laying an egg; others provide food as the larva grows, showing early traces of social behaviour.

The ladybird is a brightly coloured beetle, the only beetle many people will touch. They are found almost everywhere but many of the 44 species have specialised habitats, from marshes to pine trees.

The devil's coach horse is a rove beetle, one of a large group of beetles with short wing cases. Unlike many of its species, this insect's abdomen can be clearly seen. It is black and somewhat threatening. When alarmed, it will lift its rear end and open its jaws.

Yorkshire Wildlife Trust's Fen Bog
Nature Reserve is one of the best
examples of an upland valley mire in
Britain. The post-glacial peat in the
valley bottom is up to 12m deep. Almost
900 species of flora and fauna have been
recorded on this combination of mire,
wet heath and moorland. A mixture of
wet and dry areas on the reserve
encourages a wide range of plants,
including ten species of sphagnum moss,
cranberry, round-leaved sundew, bog
myrtle and heath spotted-orchid.

Allerthorpe Common, a superb example of lowland heath, is another Yorkshire Wildlife Trust Nature Reserve and a particularly good place to see adders and lizards. In a small area, just 6.5 hectares, there is a range of habitats which has encouraged a rich variety of invertebrates; records include over 200 species of moth and 150 of spider. There are water beetles in the ponds and dazzling dragonflies darting around above the water – particularly species such as the four-spotted chaser, blue-tailed damselfly and black darter.

This damselfly, beautiful demoiselle, is similar to the banded demoiselle. In the male beautiful demoiselle, the colour covers the whole wing; females are harder to separate but the beautiful demoiselle has broader wings, with a brownish appearance.

Found mainly in the west of Great Britain, bog myrtle can also be seen in Yorkshire. A low, spreading shrub growing up to two metres high, it is deciduous and produces catkins in spring followed by sage-coloured leaves. The plant is used to flavour gin.

Mating azure damselflies. A beautiful sight during the summer, the azure damselfly prefers still or very slow flowing water. Damselflies are smaller than dragonflies and prey on smaller insects. When at rest, their wings rest above the body, unlike dragonflies, where the wings are straight out.

From a tuft of submerged leaves, the water violet's lilac flowers sit on a single stalk rising 30-40 cm from ponds and ditches. Its roots do not need to reach the bottom of the ditch but draw nutrients from the water.

Grass and farmland

Roseberry Topping. This distinctive hill, an outlier of the Cleveland Hills, owes its shape to 19th century ironstone mines. The climb up the grassy slopes by the bluebell-filled oak woods is well worth the effort for a view from the rocky summit across the surrounding farmlands of the vale of Cleveland to Teesside and County Durham.

In Britain, grasslands would occur naturally in only a few places, such as on exposed clifftops and on mountains. Most have been created by man clearing woodlands to keep livestock as agricultural society developed.

Today grasslands are important for a huge range of flora and fauna. Species found in any area will depend on the type of soil – whether it is limey, neutral or acid – on nutrient and moisture levels, and on the way land is managed.

Wildflowers can transform grasslands into an astonishing sight when they are in bloom, but overgrazing or undergrazing will prevent important species from flourishing. Careful management, ensuring stock are on the land in the right numbers at the right time of year and cutting grass for hay after the seeds have set, will ensure flowers come again year after year.

As well as plants and flowers, many ground-nesting birds also need grasslands – in Yorkshire skylarks and meadow pipits will be seen on drier areas; snipe and shelduck breed where it is wetter. Butterflies, such as meadow brown and ringlet, are also dependent on this habitat being maintained and managed carefully for them.

Most grassland has been created by farming and farming continues to have a huge impact on wildlife in Yorkshire.

Rabbits were introduced to Britain by the Normans in the 12th century to provide meat and fur. They live in extended family social groups in networks of tunnels, dens and bolt-holes known as warrens.

Brown hares are often seen running across open farmland and can reach speeds of up to 45 mph. Young hares, called leverets, are born in shallow scrapes in the ground known as forms. They rely on camouflage and remain motionless to avoid being preyed upon.

Opposite. Found throughout the world, the barn owl, with its ghostly shape, moves silently and low over grassland, hunting for voles, mice and other small mammals, using its excellent hearing to find its prey. The forward edges of the primary wing feathers are not smooth like most birds, but serrated; this reduces the noise made in flight to almost nothing and allows the owl to approach unnoticed. Hearing is enhanced by the evolution of the ears and the feathers round the face, which allow it to identify exactly where a noise comes from.

The rhythmic song of the yellow-hammer, 'little-bit-of-bread-and-no-cheese', is one of the most recognised, and is a familiar sound on spring walks through farmland. Since they usually sing from an exposed perch, yellow-hammers are frequently seen and easily identified. They like to nest in hedgerows and can be threatened by changes in farming practice.

One of winter's colourful visitors, the fieldfare is seen in large flocks in wood-land trees and hedgerows or feeding in grassland. Chaucer called them 'frosty feldefares', as they are seen in the worst winters, migrating from Scandinavia or Russia, along with flocks of other wintering birds such as redwing and brambling.

Corn buntings are not common in Yorkshire but visitors watching seabirds on the Yorkshire coast may well see them if they turn round to view the fields behind them. Although their plumage looks lark-like, corn buntings are from a different family. They depend on seed and grass heads for year-round food, so farming techniques can affect populations.

Tree sparrows look similar to house sparrows and the two are often mistaken. They can be identified by their red-brown head and the black cheek patch surrounded by white, hence the Yorkshire name, red-headed sparrow. This species has suffered a major decline, with populations falling by over 80 per cent since the late sixties.

Just as birds, such as the robin, will follow a gardener round the vegetable patch on the look out for worms in newly dug soil, so this flock of gulls follows the farmer across the field ready to snap up anything exposed.

Turning hay at Drebley with Simon's Seat in the background. The cutting of hay after wildflowers have set seed means that the flowers have a chance to grow again the following year.

Fields of crops such as wheat and barley can provide a favourable habitat for many of our native species. However, intensive arable cropping based on heavy doses of inorganic fertilisers, fungicides and weedkillers has eroded wildlife habitats on the chalk wolds. There are concerns about nitrogen pollution of the groundwater and drinking water, the losses of farmland birds like the grey partridge and the cost of arable subsidies to the taxpayer. Public policy on agriculture is a major influence on wildlife in our countryside.

The harvest mouse is the smallest British mouse and spends much of its time aloft in the tops of tall stems of grasses using a prehensile tail like an extra limb to enable it to cling to even the most slender stalk. It makes aerial ball-shaped nests out of woven blades of grass in which it lives throughout the spring and summer months and in which up to eight young will be born. When autumn approaches, the harvest mouse moves down to ground level and spends the winter months living in tunnels just below the surface, surviving on food it has collected and stored.

Found in hedgerows and woodlands, the slender stems of stitchwort with their white flowers can vary considerably in height. Traditionally, this plant was powdered, sometimes added to wine and used to ease pains or 'stitches' in the side.

The stoat is the larger cousin of the weasel, being almost twice the size. It also has a distinctive black tip to its long tail. In severe winters the stoat's fur may change colour, becoming pure white, but the tip of its tail always remains black.

Coverdale, like other Yorkshire dales, used to be cloaked in woodland. This has been cleared over the centuries, leaving tell-tale signs like bluebells growing in the open. The open stretches of meadow provide a perfect hunting ground for birds such as the little owl which can scout for prey from the branches of trees dotted here and there. Small mammals can take refuge in the tall grass.

In May and June, the delicate flowers of ragged robin, with their split petals, are striking, especially when growing in numbers – usually in fairly wet conditions. They are mostly deep pink, though occasionally a white flower can be seen. The leaves feel slightly rough to the touch.

Vetches are part of the pea family and this can be seen easily when they flower. Although there is a wide range of sizes and colours – seen here is the meadow vetchling – a close look shows they are similar to garden varieties.

Cursed by gardeners for seeding everywhere and being difficult to uproot, dandelions are a successful wildflower because of these very qualities. They are more popular with Yorkshire's wildlife, such as hoverflies.

The cowslip's leaves form rosettes at the base of the plant. From here rise the stems or 'scapes' which bear the strongly coloured yellow flowers, sometimes up to 30 on a single scape.

Most plants survive by converting sunlight to energy. The chlorophyll required to do this is not found in fungi. They take their energy from living or dead plants. As well as the visible part of the fungus, which will distribute spores, there is an unseen network of hyphae, hairlike strands, which gather nutrition.

Despite its appearance, the slow-worm is not a snake but a lizard, feeding mainly on worms, slugs and snails. When not feeding, it can be found either basking or hiding under stones. Like other lizards, it has the defensive protection of being able to shed its tail by contracting muscles to fracture one of its vertebrae, allowing it to escape a predator.

Yorkshire's most common bird of prey, the kestrel, is seen regularly throughout the county. It hunts for small mammals, especially voles, often on motorway verges. Even without sight of the plumage, a kestrel is easily identified by its distinctive hovering flight. Wings and tail keep moving in the wind, adjusting, so that the head stays still, watching for prey, before swooping down.

This winter visitor is often seen in large flocks, sometimes with the slightly larger fieldfare. Part of the thrush family, the redwing's rust-red patch is visible when it is spotted in trees or on the ground but it is even more distinctive when seen in flight. As it uses up winter food supplies, the redwing often moves from the countryside to town parks and gardens.

Right. It is difficult to imagine that a hundred years ago, this now common, hibernating, garden butterfly was virtually unknown in Yorkshire! The peacock has had a few ups and downs since then, but is still increasing its range and beginning to appear in some of the highest gardens in the county. Big 'eyes' on the underside of the wing are used to frighten enemies, sometimes in combination with a squeaking noise made with the wings.

Below. The orange tip is a common springtime butterfly, often seen along roadsides because it lays its eggs on common hedgerow plants like garlic mustard. Only the male has the bright orange wingtips. The female is mainly white and easily mistaken for the common small white butterfly, except for her lacy-patterned lower wing.

Opposite. A wildflower meadow in Swaledale. As more and more flower-rich meadows have been lost to agricultural intensification those which are left have assumed a much greater importance. Many have been designated as nationally important Sites of Special Scientific Interest giving them special protection, and grants are available to farmers to encourage benign management. Without cutting these meadows would soon lose their diverse flora. It is only through the continuing good stewardship of the Dales farmers that they flourish for all to enjoy.

Muker, Swaledale. Sheep and cattle have played an important part in the formation of the Dales landscape. Careful grazing keeps down vegetation and can preserve wildflower meadows. Drystone walls which keep animals enclosed and barns which shelter them over the winter have created the characteristic barn and wall landscape we know today. The walls provide a refuge for small mammals and a hunting ground for the wily stoat. Isolated barns serve as nesting sites for endangered barn owls, who quarter the surrounding meadows at dawn and dusk, silently hunting for unsuspecting field voles.

Below. For generations, flower-rich meadows have been cut in summer to provide winter food for stock. Timing of the first cut is traditionally set, not by the calendar, but by a small plant called yellow rattle . When the seeds of this plant rattle in their pods it is time to reach for the scythe or tractor keys. The hay can then be used to feed the livestock through the winter months. Yellow rattle is an annual plant, needing to spread seed every year to survive.

Moorland

Hawnby Hill and Moor. The vast stretches of heather on Yorkshire's upland moors, wet deserts to some, haunt of curlews and merlins to others, have been maintained by a combination of burning and sheep-grazing, without which the moors would probably revert to oak and birch forest. However, over-grazing can damage the balance leading to the encroachment of bracken and to soil erosion. Upland farmers are now being encouraged to stock the land at lower densities.

Many people think of moorland as being a typical Yorkshire habitat, remembering visits to the North York Moors, parts of the Dales, even the upland areas close to West Riding cities and towns. But very little of Britain's moorland is natural. Unlike the Flow Country in Caithness in the north of Scotland, in Yorkshire, moorland is semi-natural.

Much of the landscape which is now moorland was once woodland. But as agriculture began to replace hunting and gathering great areas of trees were cleared. Soil conditions and natural drainage made agriculture on the hills possible but trees could not regrow because animals grazed these areas. Any new shoots were quickly eaten. The species of plant which grow there are native but man created the conditions which allowed them to flourish. Their cycle of growth and die-back has created the thin peaty soils characteristic of moorland.

The vast stretches of purple heather which characterise much of Yorkshire's moors remain in this familiar condition only because of man's intervention. Since Victorian times, keepers have managed moorlands for shooting, trying to increase numbers of red grouse. Burning is used to maintain a patchwork of heather at different stages of its development: young growth on which the grouse can feed and mature growth in which the bird can nest and hide. Grazing by sheep keeps the balance between heather, scrub and grass. If too many sheep are grazing on a moor, this balance can be lost, as hardy breeds, like Swaledales, can graze heather throughout the winter, reducing its acreage.

With careful management, Yorkshire's moors will continue to be a distinctive part of the county's landscape.

The short-eared owl is frequently seen by birdwatchers and walkers as it hunts during daylight. Found on moorland during summer, it migrates to lower ground during winter. The ear tufts which give it its name are not always seen but usually raised when the bird is disturbed.

The red grouse's impact on estates in the county can be seen from the many Yorkshire names for the bird: moor bird, moor cock, moor hen, moor game and moor poot. It is difficult to walk over any Yorkshire moor without being startled by a grouse flying noisily away after being disturbed. The raucous 'kuck-kuck-kuck' call gradually fades as it flies to a safer spot.

The clint and grike formations of limestone pavements are one of the most characteristic features of the Yorkshire Dales – clints are the blocks of limestone, grikes are fissures between them. Great care is required when walking along clints. Yorkshire Wildlife Trust's Southerscales Nature Reserve, on the north-west slopes of Ingleborough, and South House Pavement on the east, are ideal places to see limestone pavement and the important plants it supports, including baneberry, lesser meadow rue, hairy stonecrop and twelve species of fern. Rigid buckler fern, hart's tongue fern and polypody can all be found. Such areas are not particularly habitable for birds but are nevertheless frequented by upland species such as wheatear, meadow pipit and ring ouzel.

The pee-wit call of this favourite bird is very easily recognised – the black, white and green plumage with the crest making it easy to spot. A ground-nesting bird, the young lapwing can run almost as soon as it is hatched in case it needs to seek shelter from predators.

Easily spotted by its almost rectangular wing shape, the lapwing can be seen in huge flocks in winter. In spring, however, it pairs up and can be found on moorland and wet grassland. A great aerial entertainer, it uses flight displays to fend off rivals; steep climbs and dives, mixed with graceful swooping, are part of its mating flight.

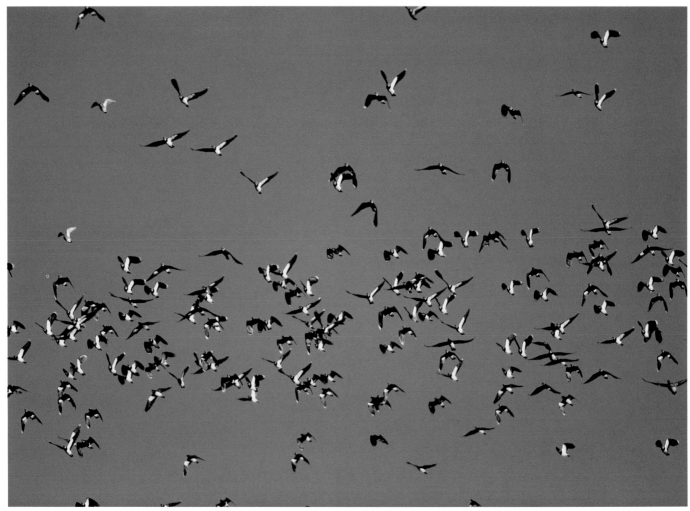

There can be no doubt where the golden plover's name came from; its breeding plumage is a black face and breast, lined with white, and a golden back. Common on Yorkshire moorlands in spring and summer, it can be found wintering at lower levels, sometimes in huge flocks, or in smaller numbers mixed with lapwing.

The golden plover is a striking moorland species. Often found with lapwing in winter flocks, it can be distinguished from it by its pointed wing-tips against the rectangular shape of the lapwing's.

A familiar sight on moorlands and wet bogs, cotton grass is not a grass but a sedge. Rhizomes beneath the surface allow it to spread into large patches, sometimes forming fields of white.

Peregrine falcons have suffered a severe decline in numbers since the Second World War, reaching a low point in the 1960s – probably because of extensive pesticide use; adults have been affected directly and in addition egg shells have become thinner with eggs often failing to hatch. They are now recovering to some extent and spreading over a wider area. Traditionally they use cliffs as nest sites but can be found in quarries, on viaducts, even buildings in cities, where they search for prey on the wing.

86

Overleaf. Westerdale in the North York Moors exemplifies the area's richness of habitat: open moors and grassland, woodland, fertile farmland and water. The perfect landscape for all kinds of wildlife.

Common buzzards are widespread in Wales, Scotland and the South-West but seen less often in Yorkshire. Even so, their wingspan and high circling flight make them an impressive bird of prey. Other species also occur in Yorkshire – the honey buzzard in summer and the rough-legged buzzard in winter – so a close check of features and a glance at a good field guide are worthwhile.

The wheatear is often one of the earliest spring migrants to arrive. It can be seen near the coast at first, then in other parts of the county, but many make their way to higher ground to breed. Wheatears winter in Africa – not only those from Britain but also birds which breed in Canada. Their non-stop flight over the Atlantic makes them one of the most impressive migrants.

Similar to stonechats, whinchats have a distinct stripe above their eye, though the male doesn't have the former's black cap and white collar. Fortunately, they sing from the tops of bushes or from posts, making it easy to get a good view of them. They can be found in different habitats – from rough pastures, wet grassland and bracken-covered slopes to railway embankments.

In the distance lies Pen-y-ghent, one of the famous Three Peaks of Yorkshire in the heart of Yorkshire's limestone country. The farmsteads and field boundaries on these uplands are built mostly from stones shifted to clear land for grazing by sheep and cattle. Far below the land surface are deep cave systems created by rainfall percolating through the porous rocks above.

The red deer is our largest deer and fully mature males, unlike the female pictured below, carry impressive, distinctive antlers. These are shed each spring and then a new set develops over the next year. Red deer are found in many parts of Yorkshire particularly the North York Moors and parkland around Fountains Abbey.

The curlew is often thought of as
Yorkshire's special bird, particularly in
the Dales. Every spring its haunting
song carries for long distances. The
display flight involves steep rises, then
long, graceful, downward glides. In
winter, away from frozen upland
ground, curlews gather in large flocks in
estuaries where their long bills can
probe for food in soft mud.

As with the puffin, the strong colours and striking bill of the oystercatcher often raise a smile from watchers. Historical records suggest it used to be found mainly on the coast but it is now common on Yorkshire's grasslands and moorlands. Its technique for opening cockles and mussels includes hammering the shells until they break and stabbing at the gap between the two shells until they part.

Embsay Moor. The result of Bronze Age deforestation and farming on thin soils, Yorkshire's heather moors are now internationally important for their wildlife, particularly breeding birds like golden plover and dunlin. Red grouse, much valued by sportsmen and chefs, however, are their most important resident. Income from shooting underpins the management of the moors. Heather honey is another greatly-prized moorland product.

Much less common than the red, the
black grouse can still be found in some of
Yorkshire's upland areas. The males
gather on traditional sites where they
will fan their tails with the bright white
under-tail coverts and defend their place
in the 'lek'. A complex series of displays,
hisses and calls, and fights with other
males, are all used to attract females.

As well as open farmland, skylarks favour moorland areas and can often be seen as a distant speck high up in the sky. Their beautiful, continuous flow of song performed on the wing is very individual and can last up to five minutes.

The nest of the ring ouzel is made from grasses and twigs set amongst rocks and crevices of the mountains and wild moorland areas it likes to inhabit. The chicks are fed on insects, berries and fruit. A summer visitor to Britain, the ring ouzel has been called the mountain blackbird as, apart from the white crescent on its chest, it is similar in appearance and behaviour.

Rivers, lakes and wetlands

Wooded waterfall, in the Rivelin valley, Sheffield. The many rivers, canals and mill ponds in and around Sheffield provide a habitat for important species including the endangered water vole and the native white-clawed crayfish. Improvements in water quality in recent years have improved the potential for creatures like the otter, once lost from the area's rivers, to make a comeback.

Water is essential for wildlife and Yorkshire's wetlands make up a varied mosaic of habitats. It is not just fish which live in this network of rivers, streams and ditches, lakes, reservoirs and ponds. Birds, plants, insects, mammals and so much more can be found too. Water also adds distinctive character to the county's landscape, attracting large numbers of walkers and picnickers, drawn to rivers and lakes.

Every river changes during its course. High in the catchment areas, springs and bogs are formed on moors; plants like butterwort and bog asphodel may well be found here. Upland rivers formed from these sources are usually cold and fast-flowing favourites of birds such as dipper and grey wagtail. As they reach lower levels, the gradients are not as steep and the flow of water slows down, a better habitat for kingfishers, marsh marigold and ragged robin. Finally rivers become tidal; estuaries often have characteristic mudflats, like the Humber, rich in invertebrates and a feeding ground during migration for thousands of wading birds, like curlew and oystercatcher.

Yorkshire's rivers have been an important factor in man's history, in the settlement and growth of towns and cities, and in the formation of industries. Wetlands can help man control the force of water, particularly during flooding. Wheldrake Ings is an example of a great seasonal wetland. During the summer it is rich in wildflowers and other rare plant species, with birds such as snipe, lapwing and redshank breeding. In winter, the River Derwent floods it, taking some of the pressure off towns and villages downstream and providing a habitat for thousands of wintering waders and wildfowl, such as wigeon, teal and pintail.

After spending between four months and three years in water as a nymph, mayflies emerge for the last, short stage of their life. Many are eaten by fish but the lucky few reach waterside plants. They have upto four days of life in which to mate. This can sometimes be seen happening in swarms over water in the evening; the females then lay eggs in the water after sunset.

Marsh marigolds, or king cups as they are also known, favour wet areas such as marshes, fens and reed beds and are often seen along Yorkshire's river banks. Although its petals were once used to colour butter, the marsh marigold is poisonous.

The largest British fish found only in freshwater, pike can grow over a metre in length and have elongated heads with curved teeth to prevent their prey escaping. This young pike will eat insect larvae but, as its grows bigger, will feed on fish, especially perch, birds such as moorhen and ducklings, and even small mammals.

The colourful sight of a kingfisher along the county's rivers is a great favourite with many people, even if it is only in the form of a blur of azure blue and orange. Birdwatchers near water listen for the kingfisher's call – a whistling sound – which often precedes its arrival. The bird can be spotted on a convenient perch, studying the water for prey, completely still until it dives suddenly and almost vertically. Once young birds emerge from the nest tunnels excavated by the parents in the river bank, it is possible to see several birds perching close together.

Following a widespread national decline during the sixties and seventies the European otter disappeared from much of Yorkshire. Since then the population has been recovering slowly thanks largely to the work carried out by Yorkshire Wildlife Trust's Water for Wildlife project. However, there is still a long way to go before they are breeding successfully on all rivers. While threats associated with pollution and persecution have been reduced, many pressures still remain from development, agricultural changes, flood defence, mineral extraction and, of course, traffic.

The small cave spider is found in caves, cellars and other dark places. Like many other of its species, it spins a web to catch passing insects and produces spherical sacs full of eggs, which it hangs with thick silk.

The water vole is Britain's largest vole, measuring up to 30cm from nose to tail tip. Immortalised as Ratty in Kenneth Graeme's children's classic, *The Wind in the Willows*, sadly the water vole is no longer a common sight in our rivers, canals, streams and ponds. Loss of habitat, drainage of wetlands and increased predation by the introduced American mink have all contributed to the disappearance of this charming and inoffensive small mammal.

Easy to see why the River Swale, seen here at Richmond, is often referred to as 'swirling'. Fast flowing after rainfall, as it sweeps downhill on course to join the Ouse, stained brown by peat picked up from moorland springs, it is a favourite habitat of dippers and wagtails. The Swale is once again home to otters – one of Yorkshire's great success stories.

The white water lily's deep green leaves usually float on still or slow-moving water but sometimes are held just above the surface. Although large, they do not cover enough of the surface to cut out all the light needed by other species. In summer the show of white flowers make Yorkshire's lakes and ponds even more attractive. At night the flower may sink below the water, to rise again next morning.

WILD YORKSHIRE

The monkey flower is a North American native, now naturalised in Britain. Its large yellow flowers have small spots of red. Popular in gardens, it can also be found in marshes, by streams and the margins of lakes.

Strongly aromatic, water mint will grow in a wide range of wet places. The pink flowers are just 5mm long but occur in dense rectangular heads. As the stems continue to grow, the heads can split into whorls, leaving rings of flowers lower down the stem.

Grey herons can be found all over Yorkshire either hunting in shallow water or in flight. Their huge wingspan, with a long, slow wing-beat, makes them easy to pick out. In spring they congregate in a heronry where hundreds of pairs come to the same spot to breed. One of the best places to see them raising their chicks is Yorkshire Wildlife Trust's Bretton Lakes Nature Reserve, near Wakefield.

The brown spikes of the reedmace (also known as bulrush), appearing in June or July, sometimes over two metres in height, are the developing seed heads, which will stay on the plant until the following February. The grey-green leaves, about 20mm wide, are as easily spotted as the seed heads but the tiny flowers – yellow male and red-brown female – are less often seen, except by keen botanists. The plant's rhizomes also spread out, to create larger clumps.

Cascading water tumbles 30 feet at
Falling Foss in the spectacular setting of
the Little Beck valley near Whitby.
Many of the steep-sided valleys in this
area avoided clearance and provide a
home to a rich variety of woodland
plants and animals. Some of the last
evidence for dormice in Yorkshire came
from nearby. The dormouse likes
interconnected branches of trees like
hazel and ash to avoid the risk from
predators on the ground.

The River Wharfe is seen as the gateway to the Yorkshire Dales by the inhabitants of the densely populated towns and cities of West Yorkshire. As visitors drive or walk upstream from Ilkley, the landscape becomes more and more beautiful and dramatic. Dales villages, like Kettlewell, become busy on summer weekends but the footpaths soon lead to quieter upland spots, where the views carved by glaciers and centuries of farming are best enjoyed. Kingfishers, dippers, grey wagtails and common sandpipers are just some of the many species which can be spotted along the river.

This common bird can be missed by the casual observer, since little grebes, or dabchicks as they are also known, prefer to hide in reeds or foliage for much of the time. Even when they are on open water, they spend much of their time under the surface feeding and, if threatened, will hide below it with just head and neck looking out.

Anyone who has seen this bird can have no doubt about its name, the dipper. It perches on rocks or river banks, dipping or bobbing up and down looking for beetles and insect larvae beneath the water. Birds can be seen flying close to the river's surface, bobbing on a convenient stone and then disappearing under water to reappear some time later, quite a distance away. The dipper is a fairly common sight among the fast-flowing upland rivers of the Yorkshire Dales.

Reservoirs make up much of the open water in the Dales and West Yorkshire. Embsay, and the nearby Upper and Lower Barden Reservoirs, are nest sites for over 1000 pairs of black-headed and lesser black-backed gulls. In winter, any of the larger gulls may be seen there and occasionally rarer ones, such as Iceland or glaucous. Around the edges of the reservoirs, particularly in late summer, there may be flocks of migrants heading south, including lapwings, curlews, pipits and wagtails.

WILD YORKSHIRE

Frogs have smooth, moist skin, whereas toads are warty, with dry skin. The common frog is the only native species – the edible and marsh frogs have been introduced. In October, frogs hibernate in a muddy patch at the bottom of a pond or ditch and emerge in February.

At spawning time, it is the male's voice most often heard, when it swells its throat to croak, hoping to attract a mate. There is no courtship. A male will grasp a female and she will shed as many as 3000 eggs which the male will fertilise. The eggs sink to the bottom, rising to the surface once the coating of a jelly-like substance has swollen to form the familiar frogspawn. Little of this will survive to become fully grown frogs; most will provide food for other pond life, such as fish and newts, and birds.

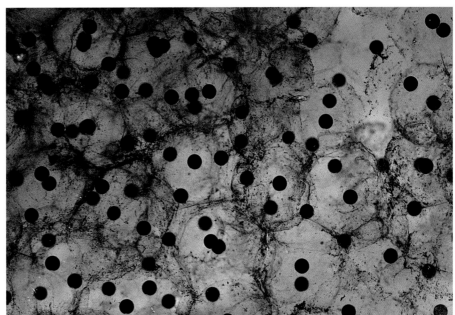

The pintail is a winter visitor to Yorkshire and one of its most elegant ducks. It has a long, narrow neck which is made to look even longer by a stripe of white which runs up from the breast to the head. The pointed 'pin' tail is also long and distinctive. Pintails occur in small numbers compared to other wintering wildfowl but can be picked out in huge flocks in wetlands such as Yorkshire Wildlife Trust's Wheldrake Ings Nature Reserve.

The crayfish is Britain's largest native crustacean, about 100mm in length. It feeds on snails and insect larvae, mainly at night, finding hiding places under stones or in banks during the day. When threatened it can move very quickly by flicking its tail. It needs water which is high in oxygen and does best in hard water where the lime which it contains helps its shell develop strongly.

Below. Extinct in Great Britain in the last century, the avocet is living proof that work to create and enhance wildlife habitats can be successful in encouraging rare species. The avocet returned to East Anglia and has spread along the south coast and north towards Yorkshire. It wades through quite deep water, sweeping its long upturned bill from side to side, collecting invertebrates.

Malham Tarn, lying 380 metres above sea level in the heart of Yorkshire's high limestone country, was formed by glaciers in the last Ice Age. It is now a national nature reserve and has fresh water systems of international importance. The tarn is particularly rich in submerged plants especially spiked water milfoil and shining pondweed. Surface species include dark-leaved willow, bog rosemary and spring cinquefoil.

Woodland

Beechwood, Bolton Abbey.
Bolton Abbey and Strid Wood
provide some of the best loved
woodland in Yorkshire. The river in
the valley, grassland alongside and the
surrounding moorland combine with
the woodland to provide a range of
fascinating habitats close together.
Beech grows well in Yorkshire but is
not a natural species. It has, however,
flourished since it was first planted
and its success belies its origins. Beech
grows high and tall, often cutting the
light for other plants, so that there are
few low-growing species in the
understorey.

Woodland is the natural habitat for most of Britain, but since the Stone Age, man has cleared vast sections for his own use. Many of today's remaining ancient woodland areas are found on steep hillsides where the land could not be farmed and where it was difficult to remove the timber.

Town and city dwellers are often not far from woodland as much of it lies close to suburbs. For rural communities – in the Dales, for example – most woodland has been cleared, leaving isolated patches, such as Grass Wood near Grassington, although over the centuries there has been new planting. Planted, rather than ancient woodland, often surrounds Yorkshire's great country houses, such as Castle Howard. In the last century, this was dominated by large areas of conifers, which have now matured. These do not have the ground flora and open aspect of broad leaved woodland but rides can attract an interesting variety of plants and butterflies.

Broadleaved woodland is particularly species-rich providing a range of levels on which wildlife can feed and nest, a variety of foods and plenty of cover in which to hide. Plants also flourish; many, such as blue-bell and wood anemone, bloom in the spring before the spreading tree cover cuts out most of the summer sun.

The woodlands along the Wharfe at Bolton Abbey are a favourite place with birdwatchers especially in winter when resident species are easy to spot. In spring, migrants arrive and the woods are one of the best places in Yorkshire to watch pied flycatchers and wood warblers as they sing to establish their territory and attract a mate. As the trees come into leaf, birds become much harder to spot in the dense foliage.

Primroses are found in many different habitats, including woodland, where they prefer open areas. In the west of the country they have been known to flower soon after Christmas but are seen later in Yorkshire. They have become a popular garden plant.

Yellow archangel is a strong smelling plant, found in woodlands and shady coppices, preferring heavy clay or chalk soils. Its yellow flowers are formed in whorls along the upper stem, just above leaf nodes. The leaves grow in pairs right along the square stem.

The scent of wild garlic fills some Yorkshire woodlands in spring and becomes even stronger when the plant is crushed. It used to grow in hedgerows and farmland but was unpopular with farmers and their customers, as it could flavour milk if cattle ate it in large quantities.

The wood anemone lightens up many old open woodlands and coppices in the spring before the trees come into full leaf. The flower can sometimes be seen in old meadows and fields where it is a good indicator of previous old woodlands long since cleared. Although usually white, some flowers have purple markings which have led to their development as garden plants. Also know as windflower, wood anemones are named after the Greek for wind, *anemos*.

Robin's pincushion is a spherical growth found on roses and is caused by the larvae of the small gall wasp which lives in the hardened centre of the gall. It is green at first but turns reddish in autumn.

Despite their colouring great spotted woodpeckers can be difficult to see as they search for food. Often heard drumming in woodlands, they are most easily spotted flying between trees with a straight undulating flight. Long tongues, tipped with small barbs and sticky saliva to pick out insects, allow them to probe into the holes they have pecked.

The widespread green woodpecker, found in woodlands and open countryside, is less likely to be heard drumming than calling. Its well-known 'yaffle' sounds like laughter and can be heard from some distance – indeed, the bird is sometimes known as the yaffle. As well as in trees, it can also be seen on the ground, often feeding on ants, gathering them with its sticky tongue.

Many insects use the oak as part of their lifecycle. Some acorns have woody distortions or growths on them with deep ridges. This knopper gall is caused by the gall wasp.

Found on dead wood, scarlet elf cups vary in size from 10 to 50mm. The neat edges become more ragged as the fungus expands. Although this specimen is edible, fungi should not be picked and eaten except by experts in identification.

A comparatively easy species to identify, fly agaric has caps which sit on white stems 10-20 mm high. The caps are rounded at first but flatten out into bright scarlet discs. The white patches on the surface can sometimes be washed off by rain. Fly agaric, which can be found near birch trees in late summer and autumn, is poisonous and used to be broken up and placed in bowls of milk to kill flies.

Yellow brain fungus occurs on dead wood, often still attached to trees. It can be found all year round but is more common in autumn. It is not edible.

In spring and summer, the brackets of dryad's saddle can grow up to half a metre across on birch, elm and sycamore trees. They are circular or fan-shaped, covered in brown scales and with flesh that is quite succulent when young but dries out with age. Dryad's saddle is parasitic and can cause white rot.

The red squirrel is our only native squirrel. Once common, it is now confined to a few sites in England including certain parts of North Yorkshire. Smaller than the commonly seen grey, it lives up to its name during the spring and summer months having bright, reddish or ginger fur and a distinctive bushy tail.

Evolution has provided the tawny owl with great camouflage. Even though it is common in Yorkshire's woodlands, it is very easily missed when roosting. Other birds will often find owls for the birdwatcher, particularly during the breeding season, as song birds such as the mistle thrush will be very aware of an owl's presence and the threat to its young. Alarm calls and mobbing actions may be used to chase the owl away and lucky birdwatchers will see it flying to a new roost.

The wood mouse – also known as the long-tailed fieldmouse – can be found in most habitats though it favours fields and woodland where it feeds on acorns and seeds. A nocturnal creature, it usually lives in underground burrows which can be complex arrangements surviving from one generation to the next.

Overleaf. From late April to early June, bluebells carpet woodlands. Their early growth and flowering means they can make best use of the sunlight which they convert to energy before the trees above are in full leaf, cutting out much of their light. They spread easily to form dense patches of striking colour.

The badger is possibly one of our best known mammals, even though many people never see one in the wild. This is due to its shy, secretive nature and the fact that it is largely active at night. Badgers are social animals, living in extended family groups underground in extensive tunnel systems with nesting chambers, known as setts.

Commonly called cuckoo pint, sometimes lords and ladies, the arum is recognised by its pale green 'spathe' which surrounds the small spike-shaped flower. The base is circled with deep green leaves.

Warmer summers seem to have contributed to a dramatic spread of this hibernating species, the comma, which can be seen in spring, summer and autumn. Thirty years ago it was almost unknown in the county. Now it can be found almost anywhere. It often turns up in gardens, but seems happiest along woodland edges and rides where it can hide away in trees.

After the arum has flowered, it forms shiny berries in small clumps around the stem. The unripe fruit is green but develops into a bright red or orange.

Once common in Yorkshire, the speckled wood butterfly disappeared in the first half of the 20th century and has only recently returned. It is now spreading steadily northward, mainly up the centre of the county, and can be seen from April to October. It is a fascinating species to watch as males use all kinds of tricks to defend territories. They have even been known to 'play dead' apparently to deceive a neighbour into thinking they are no longer a threat.

Westbeck, Goathland. Upland woods remain but only where the ever-present grazing sheep have been excluded. In the steep-sided valleys running through the North York Moors National Park, a few fragments of oak and birch woodland survive. Abundant with ferns and lichens, they are carpeted in spring with bluebells, and provide breeding sites for pied flycatchers and wood warblers. Trees around here used to be coppiced to provide charcoal in the iron-smelting industry centred on Rosedale.

The ruby-tailed wasp has a shiny green head and thorax with a bright red abdomen, which gives it its name. Flying from June to August, females hunt for the nests of other wasps. If they are not 'at home' she will enter and parasitise the larvae.

The attractive black and white of the male and brown and white of the female make the pied flycatcher a favourite spring visitor in Yorkshire woodlands, although it is more common in Wales and the South-West. It is a very active bird, seen flitting between trees, gathering food on the wing and perching to allow good views for the birdwatcher.

Above. At a glance, a flying ringlet appears to be a very dark butterfly, although, in fact, it is mainly dark brown. Formerly limited to the southern edges of the county, it has recently spread dramatically to all but the highest areas. It is commonly found in grassland and on roadside verges and woodland edges in July and can sometimes be counted in the hundreds on suitable sites. It is one of a few butterflies which fly in cloudy and even damp conditions.

Left. The bullfinch is a large member of the finch family but a very compact bird, looking almost neckless. Seen in both woodland and more open countryside, bullfinches can be unpopular with gardeners and growers, as they have been known to strip buds from fruit trees. Their preference, however, is for seeds from less treasured plants, such as nettle, bramble, dock and ash.

Thorpe Perrow Arboretum. Conservationists call on anyone planting trees to use native species, preferably ones which would grow locally in a natural ecosystem. Native species are best for wildlife which has evolved to live on them; they support the biggest range and numbers of native insects, which in turn become food for birds. The 85 acres of Thorpe Perrow Arboretum show that a great collection of trees from around the world can still be home to British birds, especially when planted next to an oak woodland. Thrushes, nuthatches, treecreepers, finches, tits and woodpeckers are all at home here, along with owls, kestrels and sparrowhawks. In spring they are joined by redstarts, flycatchers, warblers and cuckoos.

INDEX

ACKNOWLEDGEMENTS

Photography by:

Mike Coultas 15, 16, 30, 31, 80

Mark Hamblin 18, 21, 22, 29, 38, 39, 46, 58, 59, 60, 61, 67 (bottom), 73 (bottom), 81, 84, 85 (top), 86 (bottom), 87, 90, 91, 94, 98, 99, 100, 103 (bottom), 104, 110, 115, 126 (right), 127 (left), 131 (bottom), 138 (bottom), 139 (bottom)

Mike Kipling 2, 6, 12, 14 (bottom), 17, 20, 24-5, 28, 33, 44-5, 56, 62-3, 65, 66, 68-9, 76, 78, 88-9, 92-3, 106-7, 112, 113, 131 (top), 132-3, 136-7, 140-1

Helen Kirk 34

Ken Paver 37

Laurie Ramsay 9, 11, 14 (top), 19, 23, 32, 40, 41 (bottom), 42, 43, 47, 48, 50, 51, 52, 53, 54 (top), 55 (top), 67 (top), 70, 71, 72, 73 (top), 74, 77 (right), 85 (bottom), 86 (top), 93 (right), 95, 102 (top), 103 (top), 105 (top), 108, 109, 111, 114, 117, 118, 119, 124, 125, 126 (left), 127 (right), 128, 129, 130, 134, 135, 138 (top), 139 (top)

Colin Raw 64, 82-3, 96-7, 116, 120-1, 122

Ian Robinson 26, 27

Denis and Mary Sykes 8, 10, 36, 41 (top), 49, 54 (bottom), 55 (bottom), 102 (bottom)

David Tarn 75

Jon Traill 105 (bottom)

Text by:

Alice Fox, Howard M Frost, Helen Kirk, Michael Krause, Robert Masheder, Adrian O'Vastar, Jon Traill, Stephen Warburton